EWKNIKLEE MEE

Inside

CREATED
EWKNIKLEE MEE

Acknowledgments

Wow, what a journey this has been! First and foremost, I have to thank the Lord Jesus Christ. His love, grace, and mercy are the reason I've made it this far, and I'm so grateful for His guidance every step of the way.

I also want to shout out some amazing people who made this bio-zine possible:

- **My Family:** Your endless support, tough love, and those hilarious moments have been the fuel that keeps me moving forward. Your honesty has been my compass, and your pride in my successes, my greatest motivation.

- **Robert:** My unofficial editor-in-chief. Your feedback made all the difference, and I don't think these pages would look as good without you. Also, I officially owe you a lifetime supply of grapes

- **Terrance:** For marketing my crafts long before I believed in myself. You became my biggest promoter without me even asking, and that meant the world to me.

- **Heaven's Eye Photography:** Thank you for your incredible patience and making the photoshoot such a fun and seamless experience. I couldn't have asked for a better session or a better collaborator.

- **My Community/Group:** Your support reminded me that my voice matters. Every like, comment, and word of encouragement lit a fire in me to keep moving forward, even on the toughest days.

- **To YOU, the Reader:** You are the heart of this project. Thank you for opening these pages and taking this journey with me. I know this format is a little different, and I am so grateful that you chose to embrace the unknown with me.

Every moment, every challenge, and every triumph has been a snapshot of what we've accomplished together. I am endlessly grateful for the laughter, love, and lessons that have shaped this bio-zine.

"EWKNIKLEE MEE," A UNIQUE MAGAZINE THAT UNFOLDS THE EXTRAORDINARY LIFE STORY OF ALTHEA, AN INSPIRING CRAFTSWOMAN, SPEAKER, AND ADVOCATE FOR EMPOWERMENT.

THIS PUBLICATION IS MORE THAN JUST A MAGAZINE; IT'S A PERSONAL NARRATIVE WOVEN THROUGH THE PAGES OF RESILIENCE, CREATIVITY, AND TRANSFORMATION.

Beyond
Today

The room falls silent as the stage lights dim, focusing all eyes on the center where the host stands, beaming with enthusiasm. "Ladies and gentlemen," the host announces, "please join me in welcoming a truly extraordinary speaker to our stage. Not only has she transformed her own challenges into triumphs, but she also inspires thousands to do the same, embodying strength, creativity, and resilience. Give a warm welcome to an incredible craftswoman, a motivational powerhouse, and an advocate for change—Althea Holmes!"

The applause is thunderous as I roll onto the stage. As the clapping fades, my smile widens, and I begin, "Thank you for such a warm welcome! Today, I'm not just here to tell you my story—I'm here to share our story, the story of embracing every part of ourselves, the challenges and the triumphs."

"I was born with Arthrogryposis Multiplex Congenita, a condition that many thought would limit me. But here I am, living proof that the only limits that truly bind us are the ones we place on ourselves."

"My journey wasn't just about overcoming physical challenges; it was about constructing a life filled with passion, purpose, and peace. I wake up every day in a home I love, surrounded by the beauty of nature on my all-year-round porch, where I meditate, craft, and prepare for moments like these."

"You might wonder how I manage it all, Well, it involves having a thriving crafting business that not only sustains me but fuels my creativity. It involves speaking engagements around the world where I am able to connect with people like you, sharing and learning."

"I'm blessed with a partner who not only supports my dreams but stands beside me as we create a life filled with laughter, love, and meaning. We've faced challenges, yes, but together, we've turned them into stepping stones for a better tomorrow."

"As for my community work, I have been able to support and advocate for children waiting to find their forever homes. Each craft I create, each word I speak, I hope to leave a legacy of hope, resilience, and relentless pursuit of happiness."

As you wave and smile, ready to exit the stage, it's clear that your story isn't just being told; it's being celebrated and serving as a beacon of inspiration for everyone.

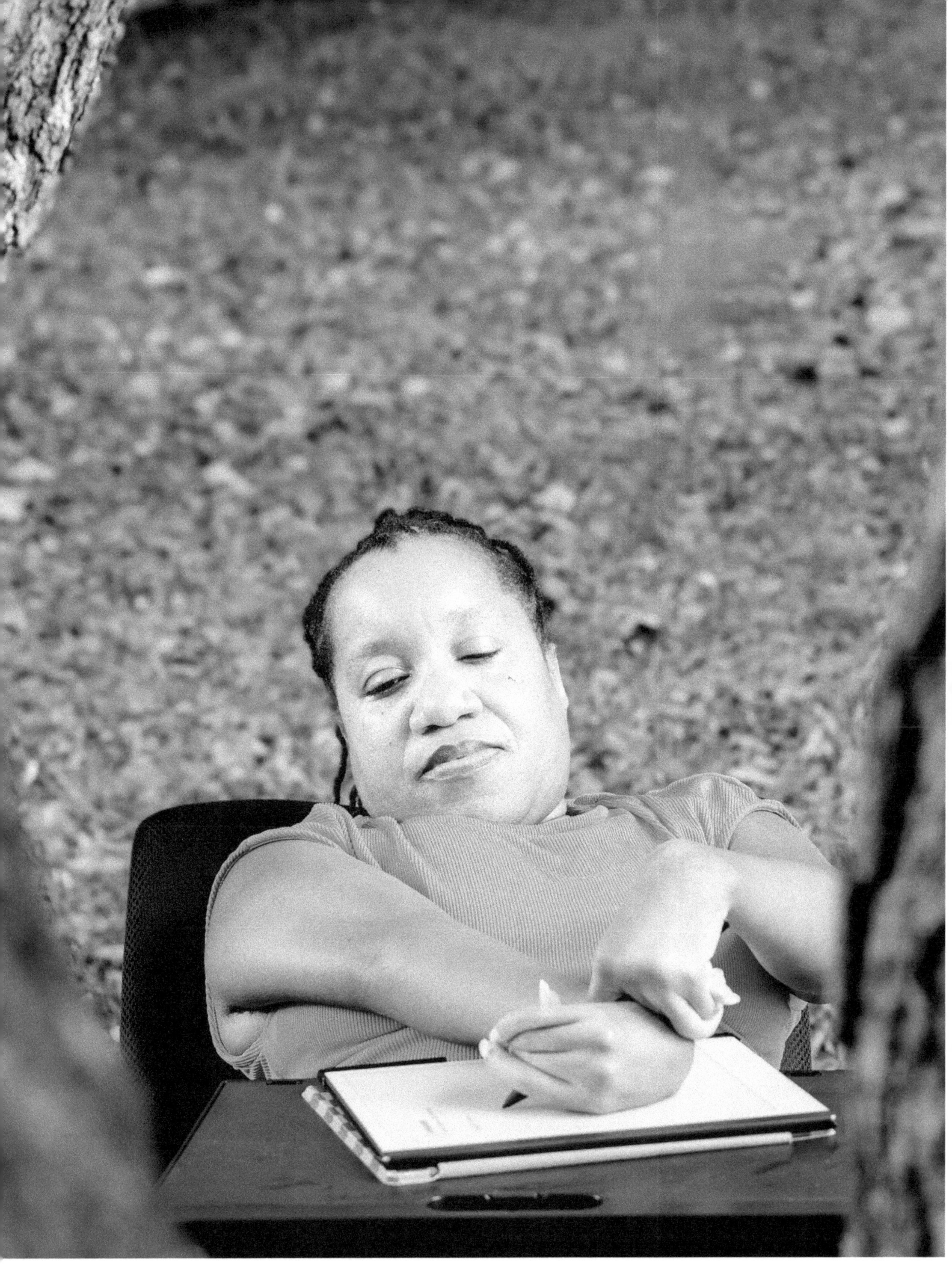

NOW
Unfolding

Today's chapter: filled with laughter, learning, and newfound passions.

Photography by:
Heaven's Eye Photography

Just a heads up, this part might feel a bit like a journal entry. I'm sort of all over the place trying to figure stuff out. I hope you can keep up and that all of this makes sense by the end.

Okay, so I have to admit, writing this chapter is super tough for me. I've been finding every excuse under the sun to avoid it. It's tricky because I honestly don't know what I'm doing. I'm completely clueless right now, and my thoughts are a total mess. Maybe breaking things down will help me sort out whether I'm actually getting anywhere.

Let's get into the toughest part—my mindset. Man, I'm seriously confused about everything! About who I am, even. Why is this even a problem? I know we're always changing, but I'm telling you, I'm totally lost! It all started spiraling after my husband Terrance passed away in 2020. He was ill for most of our time together, and I got so wrapped up in his health that I totally lost track of myself and what I liked. It took me a year or so to even start figuring out who I thought I was, but now, I'm not even sure that was right, because then I brought two amazing

little guys into my life and threw myself into homeschooling them. They were my distraction from everything else. They filled my life with laughter and joy. But then, a year later, my mom got sick and passed away in 2022. I felt numb, thinking nothing else could shake me—but I was wrong. A couple of months, 4 months later to be exact, those two boys had to suddenly move away, I completely broke down. I'd find myself crying for no reason, sometimes not eating, or just staying in bed all day. I pulled away from everyone, just wanted to wallow in my sadness.

Yup, there I was, sulking like a kid. But I couldn't keep that up for long because my best friend stepped in and gave me an ultimatum: find a therapist within a week, or she'd find one for me. Seriously, who does she think she is, right? :) But honestly i am so happy that she did. With a ton of prayer and a lot of therapy, things have started to get better. I have picked up journaling and crafting again. I have even attended a couple of events where I was a vendor selling my crafts. I was completely out of my comfort zone but I enjoyed the experiences and actually did pretty well with sells. Joining different groups that align with my interests has been impactful. I have met so many amazing

people that has motivated me to be better for myself. I am learning new skills and taking on new challenges that's keeping me on track.

So, what's next? My health, and yeah, it's definitely a work in progress. I've been trying to eat better, tossing more healthy stuff into my meals. As for working out, it's been hit or miss lately, though I used to be on top of it, even had a personal trainer and everything. One of my friends even joked, "If your trainer could see you now, he'd flip!" Guess it's time to reassess some friendships too, huh? But back to the grind—I'm aiming to squeeze in a workout two to three times a week for at least 30 minutes, but usually, I end up going longer because time just slips away.

I've got this beast of a punching machine that nearly knocks the wind out of me every time. I'm sure if I keep at it regularly, it won't feel like it's trying to end me. And I push through at least 100 sit-ups a session. Now, stretching, my least favorite exercise, is something I really need to focus on. Sitting in a wheelchair all day doesn't exactly give my limbs the freedom they need, and I know things will only get tougher with age. I've got to stay limber, especially if I want to keep up with the future I envision. No way my husband's gonna want a stiff wife, right? :)

I'm quite fortunate when it comes to my work life—I really can't complain. As an Independent Adjuster, I enjoy the flexibility to set my own hours. My work relies on natural disasters, which might sound a bit grim. However, I see

16   Continued on page 20

Me, U & Ginger, LLC

Feel the Power of Ginger – Naturally Energizing, Refreshingly Delicious!

All natural juices

For the freshest flavors, juicing season runs from March through September

Contact us today!

Otelia Robinson - Owner

678-462-1917

Admin@meuandginger.com

THE WHITE COTTON

ENTIRE HOME IN WAYNESBORO, GEORGIA

6 guests · 3 bedrooms · 3 beds · 3 baths

Great check-in experience
Recent guests loved the smooth start to this stay.

At-home coffee
Start your morning right with the drip coffee maker.

Exceptional host communication
Recent guests gave Tammie a 5-star rating for communication.

WHAT THIS PLACE OFFERS

Kitchen
Wifi
Free driveway parking on the premises
HDTV with Roku
Free washer – In-unit
Free dryer – In unit
Air conditioning
Bathtub
Private backyard
Exterior security cameras on the property

CONTACT US:

Visit Online: www.airbnb.com

THE WHITE COTTON

my role as essential—disasters happen, and people need support to recover their losses. Who better to help than me? Haha

Lately, work has been slow, which has given me the chance to focus on writing, reading, and crafting—activities I truly love. Yet, I'm always aware of the need to support myself, so admittedly, I sometimes find myself hoping for bad weather, just not nearby because I'm actually quite scared of storms! Despite the slow periods, I can honestly say that I've never been left in need. For that, I am deeply grateful.

I'm currently putting a lot of energy into building my brand, Ewkniklee Mee. This brand is all about my crafts and sharing my personal journey. I believe what I have to offer will bring a lot of joy to others, but first, I need to boost my "Con'ferdence"—as my mom used to say, LOL—and put myself out there. I'm part of this group called Stand Up, Stand Out, which is helping me get better at tackling many of these fears that are holding me back. Who knows? By the time this 'Bio-zine' hits the shelves, you might notice a "great, big, positive change in me." Please do not judge my grammar. :)

Family—what can I say? I definitely don't have a picture-perfect family, but to me, they're absolutely perfect. I'm one of nine kids, with six sisters and two brothers. Though we've lost Mother, we're blessed to still have Daddy around. I'm truly thankful for the upbringing we had. (You will get

"Sometimes, feeling lost is just the scenic route to finding yourself."

continued on page 27

20

I wanted to do something totally outside of my comfort zone so I went to the gun range for the first time with my nephew. BTW I take after my daddy Ask around! :0)

I've really grown in this area. Like the saying goes, "I'm not where I want to be, but thank God I'm not where I used to be!" Most mornings, you'll find me, listening to the Bible app, playing gospel music, or tuning into sermons. Seriously, I'm all in—taking notes, memorizing scriptures, and figuring out how to use them into my daily life when times call for it. Not all the time I use them correctly. I am stil a work in progress.

I feel like I'm getting why my parents seemed to be so excited when they were talking about The Word. My sister and I sometimes chat about what we've learned and how we plan to put it into action. It feels amazing. If I skip a day or two, something just feels off. I pray a lot more than before and try my best to stay thankful for everything I have and the journey I'm on. You know, writing this down, I realize I'm not as lost as I thought. There's real progress here. Go Thea!

27

And now, the grand finale—relationships. Oh, this part's short and sweet because, drumroll please... I'm not in one! Yep, it's just me, myself, and I right now. But hey, who needs a plus one when you've got a full life, right? (Ok I am kinda fluffing here) Maybe someday I'll dive back into the dating pool, but for now, I'm learning to enjoy the solo ride and all the personal growth that comes with it. Thanks for sticking with me through this rollercoaster of a journal entry. Here's to more ups than downs, more crafts than crises, and heck, maybe even more love down the line. Cheers to that! Haha

THE PRESENT IS THE ONLY TIME YOU OWN. LIVE, LOVE, ENJOY.

Photography by Heaven's Eye Photography

more of my childhood in a later section).

Believe it or not, about 90% of my joy and laughter comes from just being with them, chatting on the phone, or catching up over family Zoom calls. We will sometimes be up talking and laughing until daylight. It's hard to keep us separated. But it's not all laughs all the time. We're each other's toughest critics too. My family is straightforward; they tell it like it is without any sugarcoating. This honesty has shaped me into who I am today.

For instance, once I asked one of my sisters to grab me some water. Her response? "You're not that handicapped!" And honestly, I wasn't even offended—I laughed right along. Some might think that sounds insensitive, but I knew she was just worn out from work and helping around

the house. We're like that with each other—always straightforward but understanding underneath it all.

Not only do I have an amazing Dad and siblings, my nieces and nephews are one-of-a-kind! I will put them up against anyone and will choose them every time. Like what nephew do you have that will come over in the wee hours of the morning to see what is wrong with your wheelchair so you can get around and not act as if you are a bother? What niece do you have that comes to spend time with you and volunteers to clean windows? What nephews do you have to call and say, "Hey, we can we come over again and just hang?" Yea, these are my nieces and nephews. "You know, I want to share my story with the world," I say. "That's wonderful. What will you talk about because there are plenty of people rolling around here in

wheelchairs!" says my friend. HA! So as you can see, I am not spared by any of my close circles. They all keep me in check. I'm surrounded by some of the most genuine and hilarious people. I don't have a large circle, but the few friends I do have are truly remarkable. They're just as direct and honest as my family.

My best friend, in particular, is more like a sibling. We are more alike than not. We sometimes, ok most times stay on the phone for hours talking about whatever it is that comes to mind. I know anyone listening to our conversation would probably think there was something mentally wrong with us. It's not strange for our conversation to change subjects about 10 times in five minutes and but somehow we can keep up with each other.

Spiritually speaking, I've got to give myself a little pat on the back.

31

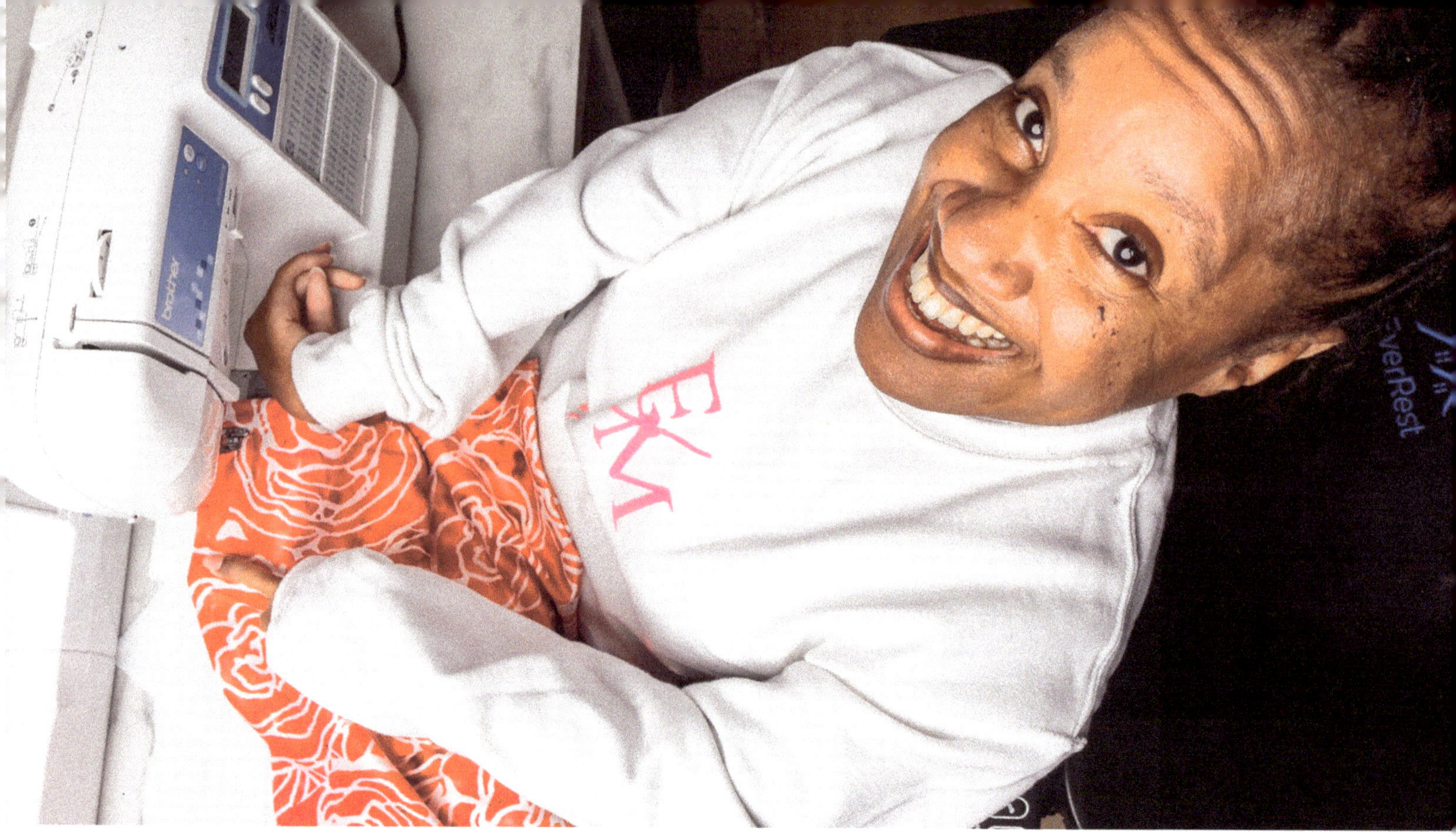

Photography by Heaven's Eye Photography

WE CATER TO MEN AND WOMEN, HANDCRAFTED WITH LOVE

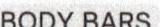 BODY BARS

 BODY MILKS

 BODY OILS

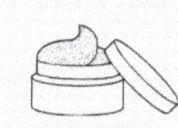 BODY POLISH

 FACIAL + BODY DEW

 BODY BUTTER

ABOUT:

Sacra +Vera redefines luxury skincare for sensitive prone skin . Indulge in our exquisite body oils, natural soaps, and nourishing serums—crafted to pamper your skin with divine fragrances and clean ingredients. Elevate your glow, naturally.

LET'S CONNECT!

 www.sacravera.com

 sacraxvera

 sacraxvera

 Sacra + Vera

Escape to Lavender Hill Bed & Breakfast, Athens' new premier boutique inn, nestled in the scenic charm of the University of Georgia's East Campus corridor. Experience the perfect blend of Southern hospitality and modern elegance in our beautifully appointed rooms. Enjoy our homemade breakfast featuring local ingredients, relax in lush gardens, and savor the serene ambiance of their rural, private setting. Whether you're here for a work event or a romantic getaway, Lavender Hill promises an unforgettable stay with unparalleled comfort and personalized service. Discover the essence of Southern charm reimagined at Lavender Hill, where every moment feels like home.

La Campagne

Special Rate: $695 / night

Plus taxes and fees (15% tax and $5/night fees per night
3 night minimum stay

- 2 bed / 1 bath
- Queen and King Bedrooms with Premium Bedding
- 55-inch Smart TV/ Spectrum Package (free Wi-Fi)
- A Sitting Area with Bluetooth Capability
- Private-detached Bath
- Complimentary Breakfast for (2) Per Day

La Ville

Special Rate: $295 / night

Plus taxes and fees (15% tax and $5/night fees per night)
3 night minimum stay

- 1 bed / 1 bath
- Bunk Bed (full over full) & Twin Sleeper Bed
- 55-inch Smart TV/Spectrum Package (free Wi-Fi)
- A Sitting Area with Bluetooth Capability
- Private-detached Bath
- Complimentary Breakfast for (2) Per Day

Booking Includes:

Complimentary Breakfast for 2 per room
Locally sourced ingredients & a varied menu including gluten-free and vegan friendly options.

Charging Station

Tesla Charging Station Available

Personalized Snack Bar

Provided upon arrival - (1) stocking per reservation per room.

 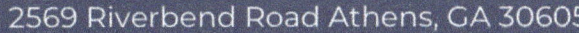 2569 Riverbend Road Athens, GA 30605

 (706) 521-2090

 www.lavenderhillbnb.com

 info@lavenderhillbnb.com

BRAVING NEW DEPTHS: *Scuba, Schooling,* AND SAYING GOODBYE

BETWEEN LOSS AND DISCOVERY: MY 2020-2023 ODYSSEY

Today's September 30, 2024, which marks seven years since I got married. It feels right to start here, on what would've been our anniversary. It's a mixed bag of emotions as I look back.

I met Terrance back in 2013, and after dating for four years, we tied the knot. From the start, his health was a battle—he had a serious episode and missed our first real date at a little art shop in Marietta. I ended up painting alone, waiting for the bus back, trying not to feel too down about it.

His health issues meant a lot of ups and downs. After we got engaged, things got tougher; he needed an LVAD implanted to help his heart work. It did help for a while, and we made the most of our time, enjoying simple things like playing games or just eating together, often in a hospital room. Our marriage was a lot about managing his treatments and frequent hospital stays. Those bus rides to the hospital, often over an hour each way, were exhausting but necessary.

Terrance was incredible, though. Even from the hospital, he was always trying to take care of me, sending me things I didn't really need but that he wanted me to have. He was all about making sure I was looked after, even arranging for help when he couldn't be there himself.

The biggest glimmer of hope came on Jan 28, 2020—a heart for a transplant was available. We were so ready for all the possibilities that lay ahead; traveling, hanging out at parks, and just being together at home. But, life had other plans. He passed away just days after the surgery on February 2nd. I will never forget, 2020 backwards.

Right when I was dealing with Terrance's loss, the world dove into the chaos of COVID. Honestly, I can't even pin down all my feelings from that time. I was heartbroken, sure, but also really scared. Scared of dying, scared of losing more loved ones to the virus. And then there was everything happening in the news, like the tragic killing of Ahmaud Arbery. It all just numbed me. I didn't know if I cared whether I lived or died. People tried to check in, but visits were off the table with everyone being so cautious. Probably for the best, because I wasn't really up for company.

I was working crazy hours then, over 60 a week, and somehow, I thought I was handling it all. But then an anxiety attack hit me hard, and it scared the life out of me. I guess I did care about sticking around after all. :) I ended up leaving that intense job for something better—less demanding

continued on page 40

and better paying.

Around that time, I started homeschooling two wonderful boys who really brought my house —and me—back to life. They got me out of bed on weekdays, and honestly, they were the joy of my weekends too. The little one, my fierce little 'protector,' would always be ready to defend me. And the older one, my 'optimist,' he could find the silver lining in anything, much like me.

These kids were with me nearly all the time for the next three years, even traveling with me. I was finally feeling normal again when my mom got sick. She fought cancer for about a year before we lost her in 2022. That hit me hard, and I fell back into numbness for a while. My mom was a huge influence on me—she always pushed me, even if it upset me, and I'll share more on that later. After she passed, I dove into therapy. I didn't want to slump back into how I was after losing Terrance. Therapy really helped, along with prayer

and journaling, and being mindful of what I listened to. I still have tough days, but I've learned not to let myself dwell too long in that dark place.

Journaling helped clear my head and made me want to get out more —meet people, travel, and try new things. Scuba diving was always on my bucket list, and I finally went for it in 2023. It was terrifying but amazing, and I might even go again, despite my fears of drinking too much ocean!

Then there was that freezing trip to Chicago to see my best friend. Why I went in the coldest season, I'll never know. My hands froze up, but we had a blast. One night, we tried to snap some photos on this gorgeous staircase in her building. It was too tough on my hands, so she grabbed pillows from the common area to help me out. We ended up laughing so hard, especially when we noticed the security cameras on us. What a night to remember!

Looking back on everything, I've really come to see how going

through such tough times pushed me to chase new experiences and find some joy again. Losing Terrance and my mom—two of the most important people in my life— really threw me into deep waters that I wasn't ready for. But, diving into scuba and getting into homeschooling these awesome kids showed me a side of myself I didn't know I had. I've come out of it not just getting by but actually learning a whole lot about life, love, and letting go. Now, as I remember this day, it's not just about the pain of the past, but also about all the good stuff I've found along the way: new strength, clearer vision, and a real excitement for what's next. Closing this chapter feels bittersweet but also hopeful. I'm ready for whatever comes my way.

BENEATH THE SURFACE OF GOODBYE LIES THE DISCOVERY OF NEW BEGINNINGS.

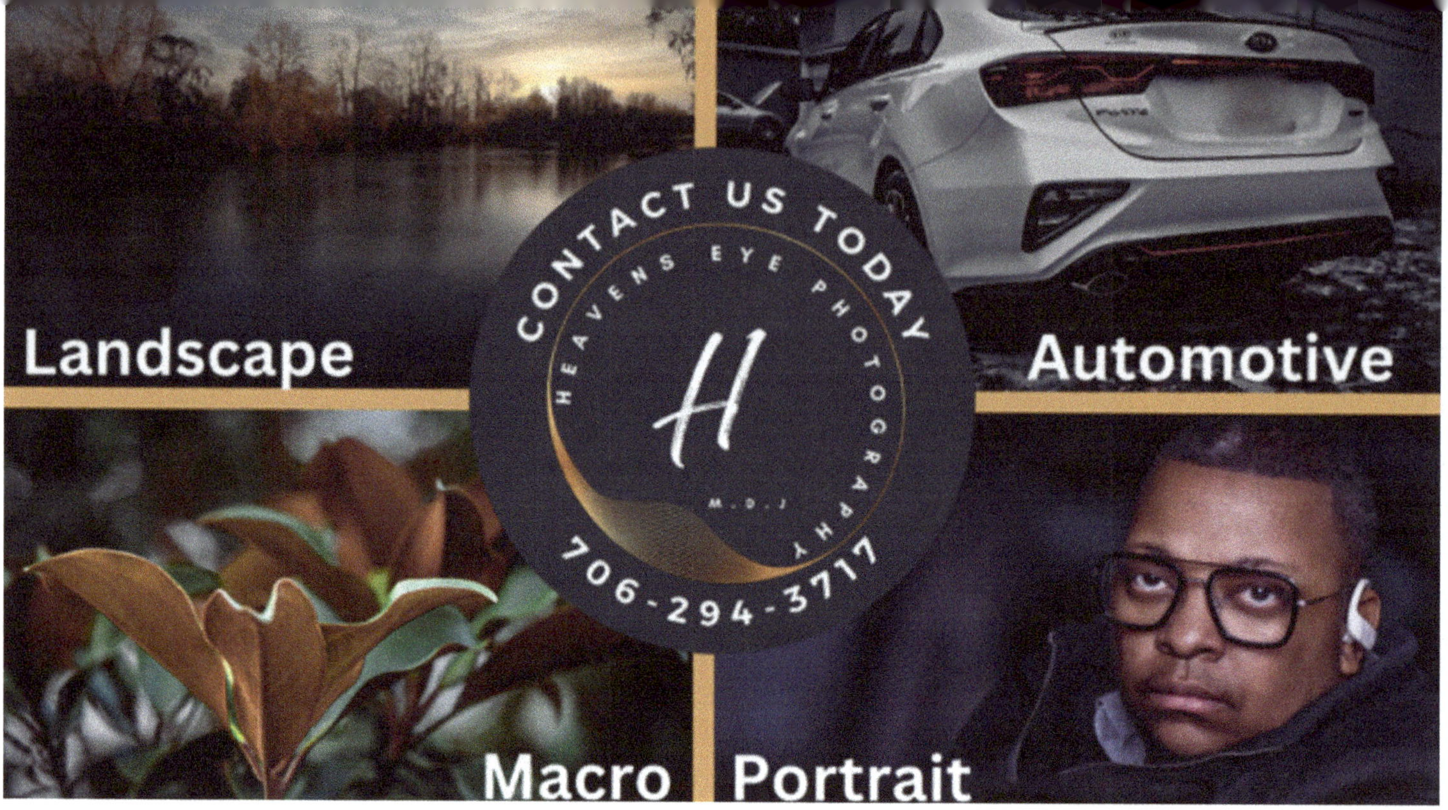

Landscape

Automotive

CONTACT US TODAY
HEAVENS EYE PHOTOGRAPHY
H
M..D.J
706-294-3717

Macro Portrait

Matthew D. Jones
Photographer

SERVICES WE OFFER

Family Portraits • Baby Showers • Birthday Parties • Retirement Events • Aerial Views and More

Looking for a custom tee or a personalized wooden sign that speaks to you? Kraftworx by Dee brings your vision to life with high-quality, unique designs. Whether it's a statement t-shirt or a beautifully crafted sign for your home, we've got you covered!

KRAFTWORX
by Dee

CONTACT US:
kraftworxbydee@gmail.com

When *the* Path Changes.

FINDING INDEPENDENCE AFTER LIFE-ALTERING DECISIONS

How are you feeling today? Any questions or concerns?" the doctor asked at my last check-up.

"Yes," I replied. "Before the surgery, I could bend forward, even clip my own toenails. Now, I can't do that anymore." I fully expected him to say something like, "You're only six weeks out from major surgery. Give it time, and you'll regain those abilities." But instead, he looked down and said, "I'm so sorry. I didn't account for how long the rod would be in your back." Stunned, I asked, "So, what can be done?"

"Unfortunately, we'll need to perform another surgery."

I was crushed. There was no way I was agreeing to another surgery, especially knowing I had only a 50/50 chance of survival with the last one. Now, I can't bend more than 45 degrees forward. This surgery took place just weeks after my high school graduation. I was so excited for it, thinking it would give me even more independence. The doctors had told me that my spine was curving rapidly, and if I didn't have the surgery, I'd likely be bedridden by the time I turned 25. Of course, I didn't want that, so I went through with it. But now, I wonder what life would have been like if I hadn't had the surgery. Would things be easier for me? I'll never know.

But I try not to dwell on that.

Instead, I focus on how I can make life easier for myself as I am now.

LEARNING TO STAND (ROLL) ON MY OWN: A LEAP INTO COLLEGE LIFE

After a few months of recovering at home, I enrolled in Columbus State University with one of my sisters. I could hardly believe I was going to college and leaving the house. I was both excited and terrified. I never thought I'd have this experience, especially because I wasn't fully independent. I needed help with basic tasks like getting dressed and cooking– things I never learned to do on my own.

I remember my mother saying often, "If you don't learn to take care of yourself, you're going to be right here at home with me and Shack!" I would think to myself, "No way!"–though I never said it out loud. Who knows what would have happened if I had! Haha Thankfully, my sister graciously stepped in to help, giving me the opportunity to further my education. But after she graduated as a nurse, she expressed her desire to travel, which hit me hard. She said she couldn't pursue her dream because she had to take care of me, and I didn't want to hold anyone back from their dreams.

I reached out to my best friend and explained how I felt. We decided to enroll at Kennesaw State together, and she would be the one to help me. This allowed my sister to pursue her nursing dreams, and I was starting to carve out my own path.

While waiting for the semester to begin, I bought some adaptive tools: a dressing stick, sock helper, button hook, and reacher–but I never used them. They were just there, unused. About a week before school started, I found out my best friend wouldn't be able to attend that first semester. Panic set in. "Oh my God, what am I going to do?" I thought. I couldn't tell my sister and ruin her excitement, so I kept quiet. She believed everything was going according to plan–she'd drop me off, and my best friend would be there to help.

When she dropped me off and helped unpack, she asked, "Are you sure your best friend is coming?" I told a little white lie (Ha) and said, "Yes, she'll be here soon."

"Okay, then, I guess I'll head out," she said.

As soon as the door closed, I cried so hard I fell asleep. The next morning, I woke up early, determined to figure things out. I prayed and looked in the closet for the easiest outfit I could manage with my tools. I settled on a black knit skirt with a little frill at the

SOMETIMES, THE PATH WE DIDN'T CHOOSE IS THE ONE THAT LEADS US TO OUR TRUE STRENGTH.

continued on page 50

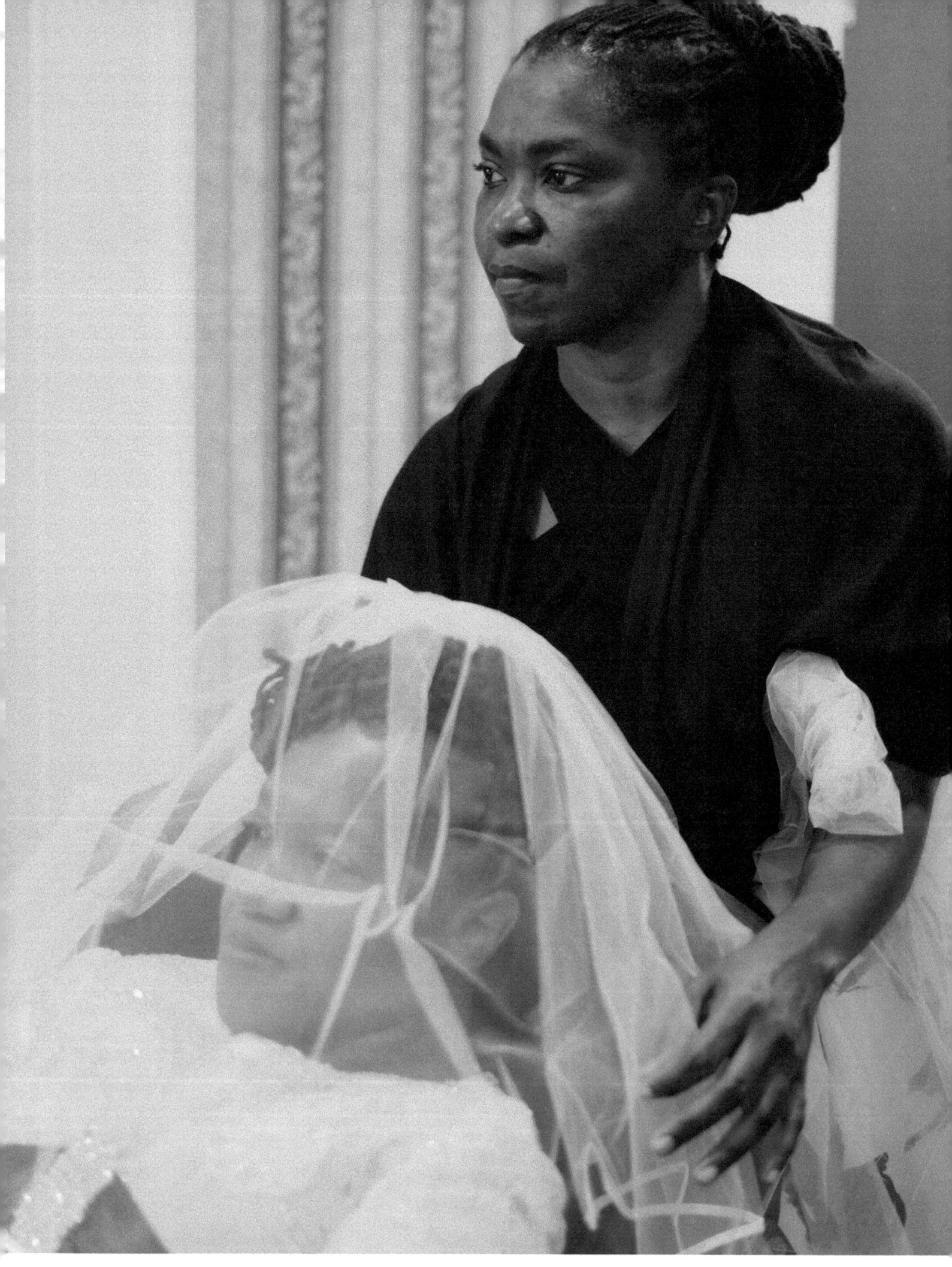

bottom, a white blouse, and a pair of socks. I don't remember the color, but knowing me, they were probably white—I had so many white socks!

Using the tools for the first time, I managed to get dressed. It took me about 20 minutes, but I felt so accomplished. I was ready for class at least an hour and a half early, and I was so proud of myself.

Next, I had to figure out food, so I decided I'd just eat at the campus café daily. The first day went smoothly. I thought, "If I can make it through this week, I'll tell my family I'm living alone."

Otherwise, I knew someone would come pick me up.

Well, I made it through the week! That Friday, I called my mom to tell her the truth. Her response was, "Well, if you think you're going to be okay, then I'm fine with it." And just like that, my journey toward independence began.

A STUDY ABROAD JOURNEY: THE HIGHS AND LOWS OF MY LONDON ADVENTURE

About a year later, I decided to take on another challenge: I signed up for a study abroad program in London. I knew London had a lot of history, and I expected many places wouldn't be wheelchair accessible. I also knew I'd have to ask for help, which I struggle with to this day, so this trip didn't exactly help me with that! :)

Two weeks before leaving, I finally told my parents. I expected them to try to talk me out of it. After all, it was my first time traveling alone, overseas, and flying! That was a big deal for me. Although they hesitated, they didn't stop me from going.

The flight was incredible, and the flight attendants took excellent care of me. When I landed in London, I was surprised to find a wheelchair-accessible taxi waiting for me. I hadn't expected much accessibility in a historic city like London, but I was wrong. Navigating London was easier than getting around in Atlanta—still true even to this day. (Atlanta doesn't make it easy for people in wheelchairs, but that's a different topic.)

The taxi took me to the dorms at the University of Westminster. The staff brought my luggage to my room, which was much larger than I anticipated but a bit outdated. Still, it was clean, and it would be my home for the next month and a half. I was thrilled to have my own room and bathroom.

Once I settled in, I explored the campus. It was so cool to see how everything was set up, with people outside playing soccer (or football, as they call it) and even cricket. What fascinated me most was hearing a Black person speak with a British accent—I'm from the country, so that was a new experience for me! :) I remember emailing my family with updates, using British lingo, and one of my sisters would reply, "Now you know you don't talk like that!" Lol, I love my family!

London was an amazing experience overall. I met so many incredible people. Many nights, we'd hang out in the common area or outside, just talking, laughing, and enjoying each other's company. We played a few games, but mostly, we just talked. I didn't need to ask for much help because everywhere I went, people offered assistance—whether it was getting me into a building, helping me with food, passing me a straw, or clearing a path so I could see.

One of the most memorable moments of the trip, though not in a good way, was the 7/7 bombings. I remember lying in bed when a student from the dorm came to my room to tell me our field trip that was planned to Bath that day had been canceled because there was a bombing nearby. I calmly said, "Okay."

"Are you alright?" she asked.

"Yes, I'm fine," I replied.

"Okay, I'll let the others know about the bombings," she said before leaving.

As soon as the door closed, I went to the bathroom, sat on the wide-rimmed toilet, and cried like a baby. All I could think was, "My parents didn't want me to come." I was terrified. We were told the trip might be extended since no one was allowed in or out of the country. Once I pulled myself together, I called my family to let them know I was okay, though the

phone reception was awful. I don't remember much else from that day, but I made it a point not to get on another train or bus for the rest of the trip. I took cabs everywhere instead. The dynamic of the trip changed after that, and I was ready to get back to Hartsfield Airport. When I did go out after the bombings, I saw security everywhere, armed with automatic weapons. It was overwhelming, so I stayed near the university for the remainder of the trip.

MY LIFE AS A M'AUNT: JUGGLING TWINS, COLLEGE, A CAREER AND FIGHTING FOR ACCESSIBILITY

About five months after returning from London, I got my first apartment—a small one-bedroom that I absolutely loved! One of my coworkers lived across the hall, and it was nice having her nearby. Sometimes, she'd come over, and we'd just eat and chat. When I was younger, I always said I wanted twins. Well, a couple of weeks after moving into my apartment, I started taking care of my twin nephews. They were a handful, but I really enjoyed having them with me. I quickly learned I could juggle way more than I thought.

My day would start with getting them dressed and off to school, then getting myself ready for work. After work, I'd come home, cook dinner, eat with them, help with homework—which wasn't always easy—then get them bathed and ready for bed. Once they were settled, I'd iron their uniforms for the next day and finish any assignments I had for school..

Growth comes not from avoiding life's obstacles, but from finding ways to thrive in their midst.

continued on page 53

I was a full-time "m'aunt," employee, and college student all at once. Looking back, I'm not sure how I managed it all. It had to be the grace of God. I kept up that routine for about three years straight.

I lived in my apartment for about two years before purchasing my first home, a cozy two-bed, two-bath condo. It was the cutest place, and the highlight was the enclosed sunroom. I absolutely loved that space—it's where I set up my desk, and I could really focus and get things done there.

After the twins moved out, I had to figure out how to fill my time. That's when I started hosting events at my place. Almost every weekend, I had people over. I was in my element, bringing everyone together to have a great time. One event that stands out was my birthday party. My home was decorated so beautifully—one of my coworkers draped sheer curtains from the ceilings and along the walls, with string lights adding a magical touch. It was stunning. I remember playing charades, laughing nonstop, and, of course, eating lots of good food.

When I wasn't hosting, we'd be out and about, hanging downtown or at Atlantic Station. It was such a vibe back then!

Years later, I moved from the condo and bought a home with some land, where I still live today. It's not a fancy house, but it's mine—a cozy brick home sitting on about ¾ of an acre. When I closed on it, though, I ran into a major issue: transportation. I couldn't get to and from work because there wasn't any affordable option. The bus either started too late for me to make it on time, or I was about ¼ mile outside their service area. It was a rough time.

I ended up staying with my sister and her family for a while until I could figure out the transportation situation. While working, I started flooding the commissioners' office with letters, advocating for better transportation options for people with disabilities. After about a year, things began to change, and eventually, I could take public transportation from work to my home.

Around that time, I also started taking driving lessons. I wanted my own vehicle so I could have the freedom to.

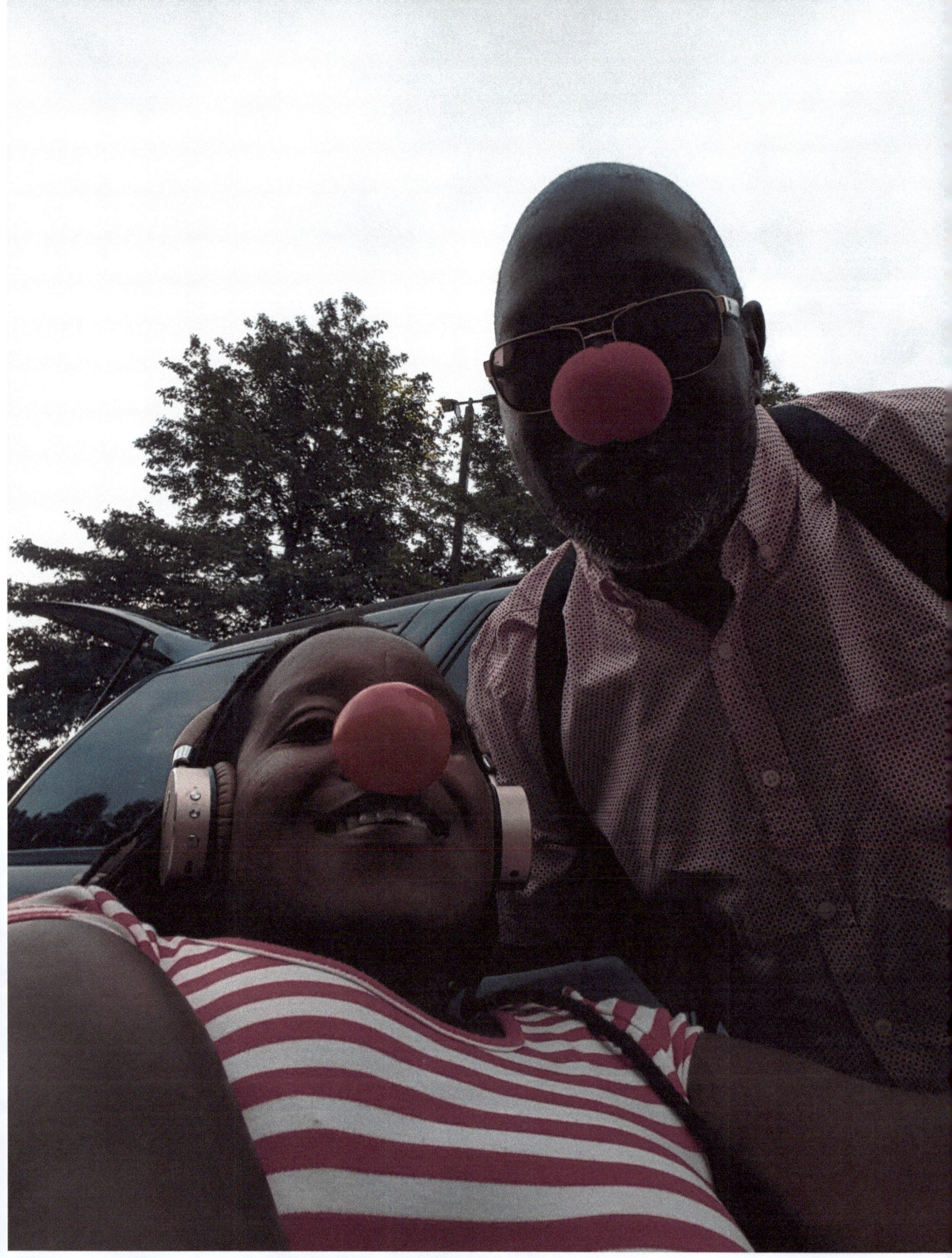

In the face of life's unexpected turns,
resilience becomes our greatest guide.

go wherever I pleased. I studied and passed the written exam, and there was a company called Freedom & Mobility that helped train me to drive using adaptive equipment. They outfitted a van with the tools I needed and gave me lessons once a week, but at nearly $300 per session, it wasn't something I could sustain for long. Still, it was a great experience. I took enough lessons to feel prepared for the driving test, but when I went to take it, I was told I needed a doctor's note clearing me to drive. Unfortunately, no doctor would sign off on it, and I never got my license. That's one dream I've had to let go of.

Now, my dream is to have a reliable driver on standby so I can go wherever I want, whenever I want. I'm going to make that happen soon.

THROUGH SICKNESS AND IN HEALTH: THE JOURNEY OF LOVING TERRANCE

About a year after moving into my home, I met Terrance online. I remember our very first phone conversation—it happened during my lunch break at work, and we talked the entire time. It felt like I had known him for years. Our first meetup was at my sister's common

area in her subdivision, so she could easily see what was happening. I was so nervous; this was all new to me.

Terrance showed up right on time, around 6 p.m., with a dozen white roses and chocolate-covered strawberries from Edible Arrangements. It was such a sweet gesture. I remember us sitting under the canopy, just talking and laughing until it was almost dark. After he left, I went back to my sister's house, and we sat around eating the strawberries. :)

We spent a lot of time together, but I noticed that he would tire quickly. He told me he had heart problems but assured me he was getting better. That wasn't true—he was actually getting worse. I vividly remember going out for his birthday dinner. As we walked into the restaurant, I headed toward the bathroom, but when I turned around to ask him to open the door, I saw him moving slowly, then he collapsed. I was terrified; I thought he had died. Thankfully, there was a nurse nearby, and EMS was called. He spent a few days in the hospital.

His health continued to decline, and eventually, he needed an LVAD (Left Ventricular Assist Device), which helped his heart

rest by taking over a lot of the work. For a while, it seemed like he was improving. We got married and enjoyed our life together, but soon, he started getting sick again. The LVAD was no longer enough. There were countless times when we'd be going about our daily life— cooking, cleaning—and his heart rate would drop so low that he'd pass out, and his pacemaker would shock him back. It was terrifying, and I never got used to it.

55

continued on page 64

EWKNIKLEE MEE
Designs

Growth is a journey, not a destination. It's the quiet persistence of planting seeds today, even when you can't see the harvest yet. It's the courage to embrace change, knowing that every challenge is a step toward something greater. Optimism is the light that guides us through uncertainty, the belief that even in the darkest moments, the dawn is coming. Together, growth and optimism transform setbacks into lessons, doubts into determination, and dreams into reality. Trust the process, nurture your spirit, and watch how life blooms in ways you never imagined.

The last time it happened at home was in early 2019. He was admitted to the hospital and stayed there until he could receive a heart transplant. While it was stressful, it was also a relief, knowing he was in the best place if something went wrong.

He ended up staying in the hospital for over a year. He never came back home. That's when life really shifted for me.

As much as I tried to prepare myself, I wasn't ready for what came next. It was like I was living in a twilight zone, waiting for a miracle, knowing that life as I knew it would never be the same. Every time I visited the hospital, I clung to hope. I prayed for healing and held onto every good day he had. But as the months passed, it became clear that his time was running out.

The day he passed, I felt a strange combination of grief and relief. He was no longer suffering, and I had to find a way to live with that. My life had been so wrapped up in taking care of him, in hoping and waiting. Now, I had to redefine everything.

Looking back, I see how those years shaped me. The challenges, the love, the loss—all of it was a reminder that life isn't always about what we expect. It's about how we respond when things don't go as planned. And despite the pain, I'm grateful for every moment I had with Terrance. He taught me that love endures, even when life changes in ways we never imagined.

Now, it's time for me to keep moving forward, to find new dreams, new joys, and new ways to live fully—just as he would have wanted."

The Strength of My
Mother's Intuition

THE BEGINNING

"That baby is going to die!"

"No, she ain't!" my mom replied. These are the words I remember hearing about my birth. I don't know much about what it was like coming into this world—no one really talked to me about my disability. I often wonder: How did my parents' lives change? Did the family dynamic shift after having a child with a disability?

I remember my mom telling me a story about when she was pregnant with me and my dad was working on additions to the house. Before she even knew there was something "wrong," she told my dad to make the doors wider. That still gives me chills—seriously, my mom must have had some kind of intuition!

A few months ago, I asked my dad what it was like for him. His response was, "It was very scary." I didn't press him any further because I could sense it's still hard for him to talk about. I also asked one of my sisters, and bless her heart, she said, "I don't remember anything, but if someone else starts talking, I'm sure it'll jog my memory." :)

I gave it one last shot and asked my older brother. He said, "I'll have to think about that. I do remember mother and daddy running back and forth to Atlanta

with you for hospital visits, and there were a lot of visits to University Hospital in Augusta too. When you got older, I remember you had to wear braces, and you cried so much that daddy had us take them off. You also had a little white bed, if I remember right. And Grandma came over a lot to help mother out with you... I really need to think more about it."

That's about all the information I've gathered about my early years. I've never seen a photo of myself as a baby, but I do remember my mother telling me I was shaped like a pretzel and could only wear cloth diapers.

EARLY MEMORIES

One of my earliest memories is going to the doctor to have a cast removed from my feet. The doctors were trying to correct the bones so I might one day be able to walk. Weeks later, I had to go back to have the staples taken out, and I remember screaming from the pain. Why am I getting emotional now? :) Get it together, Thea! Ok, on to more fond memories... Jesus. I remember being happy just playing with my two younger sisters. Though I couldn't walk, I scooted around, and them being who they are, they scooted on the floor with me. We played from sunup to sundown and they never

made me feel different. Even when it came to jump rope, I would turn the rope while the other one jumped. It was a lot of fun, especially when Daddy would join in for a short while before heading off to work on someone's car. To me, there was never anything 'wrong' with me.

If you know my family—which includes seven girls and two boys—you know we grew up in the church, and my parents didn't let us spend the night just anywhere. There was maybe one family my mom trusted. So, most of the time, we were either at school, home or at church. Church was a huge part of our lives, with Sunday morning Bible study, Sunday afternoon

67

continued on page 69

service, Sunday evening service in Augusta, and Wednesday night Bible study. Sometimes, we even had to go to the broadcast where Daddy read for the pastor. Church was life. Like it or not, we were going.

Being all that we knew, was school, church and home, most of the games my younger sisters and I played revolved around "playing teacher" as we called it and "playing church." We'd make up names for ourselves: Gan'tan, Satana, and Cassandra. No one kept the same name twice—it was all about who called dibs first! When our other siblings joined in for "play church", the fun usually moved outside. We'd create a whole setup—a bucket and a stick for the drum, an old bowl or plate as our tambourine, and another stick as the microphone. My brother would sometimes be the pastor. We had such a good time. Those were the days!

When we had services in Atlanta, it felt like we were traveling out of the country. As kids, it was a big deal—at least for me! I was especially excited to go for the General Assembly, when all the affiliate churches would come together for a week of services. We'd all be packed into our red station wagon, with a hard-top, cream-colored luggage holder on top for our bags. We'd stay at one of my mom's friends' house, who were also church members. My favorite day of the weeklong services was Sunday. That's when everyone showed up! Towards the end of the service, there would be a prayer line. I vividly remember one time when my mom was holding me, taking me up for prayer. I think we made it to the pastor, but what sticks out most is her getting happy (shouting) and sitting me right on the offering table! :) One of the deacons came over, picked me up, and held me until the service was over. Church was something special back in the day!

I also remember when Mother would go to choir rehearsal, and we'd stay with Daddy. We'd scoot around outside in the dirt, even though Mother had already told us not to get too dirty. Being kids, we did it anyway! We'd rush to take baths and sneak our dirty clothes to the bottom of the hamper like she wouldn't find out. In the words of my 4-year-old niece, "You're so silly!" :) Of course, we got a whipping when she found those dirty clothes. And yes, she whipped me too—no one was spared! :) On a recent family trip, one of my cousins shared a story about how Mother didn't play. He couldn't remember exactly what we were doing, but he got a spanking first. He said, "When it was Thea's turn, she was scooting around, screaming as she got her spanking. I had to stop crying just to watch her!" He laughed and added, "I couldn't believe she was getting a whooping too!" Lol.

LEARNING MY NAME
One memory that will forever be ingrained in my mind is the moment I figured out how to hold a pencil and write. I had one of those large red wooden pencils and a piece of brown construction paper for handwriting practice. I was sitting on the floor in my older sister's room, leaning up against her dresser, playing around with different ways to hold the pencil. When I finally got it right, I wrote my name for the first time. I was so excited!

I scooted toward the kitchen and exclaimed, "Mother, I wrote my name!" She turned around from the kitchen sink and said, "You did what?"

"I wrote my name."

"Let me see."

I proudly wrote my name again as she bent over to watch. After I finished, she said, "That is nice."

MY VOICE DIDN'T START AS MY OWN. I LEARNED TO SPEAK UP BY WATCHING THE STRONGEST PERSON I KNEW—MY MOTHER.

continued on page 71

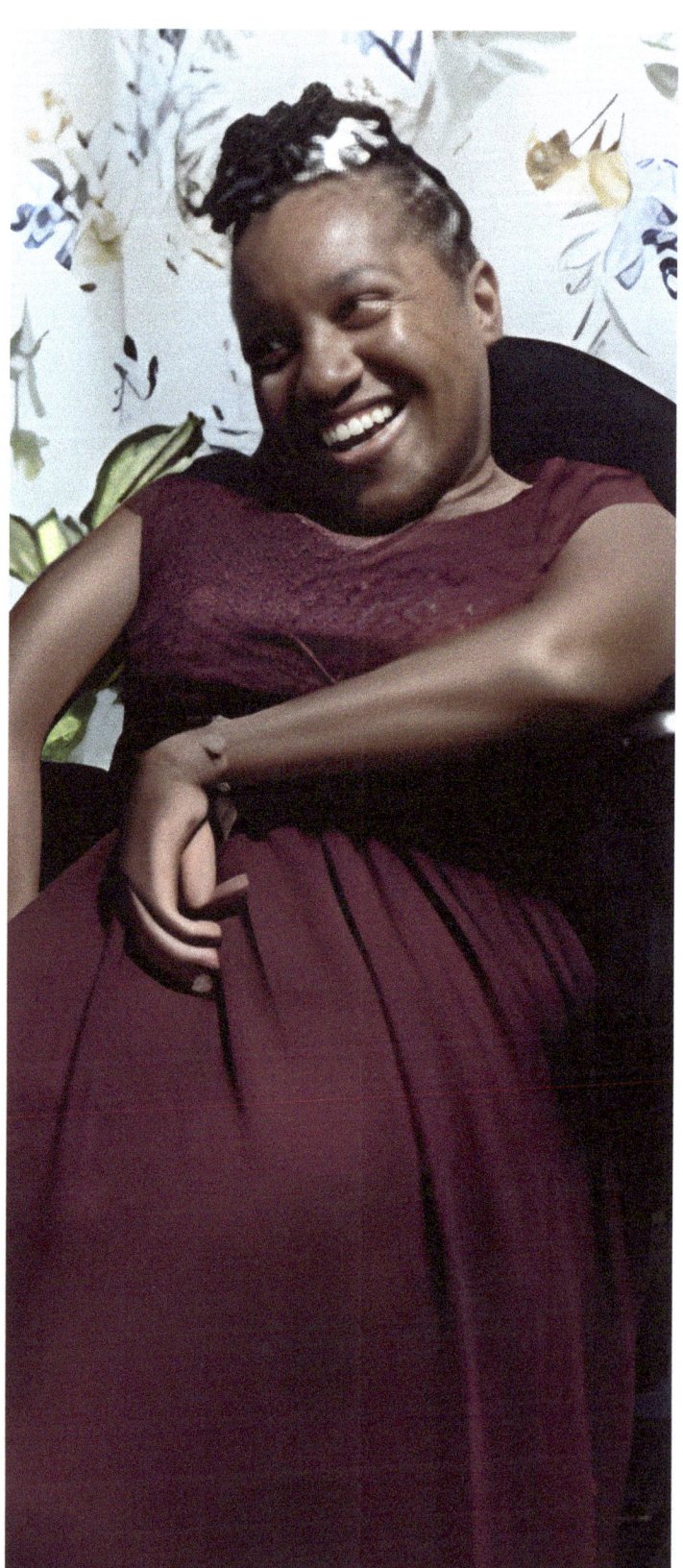

and turned back to the sink. But as she turned, I caught one of the biggest smiles on her face. I felt so proud of myself.

SCHOOL STRUGGLES AND TRIUMPHS

Enrolling in school was a big deal. The administrators initially thought I should be placed in a special education class, but my mom knew better. She came up to the school and told them there was nothing wrong with my mind—I could think just like the other kids. I think I stayed in the special education class for one day. Mother didn't play! Lol.

Overall, school was fun for me. I had a lot of friends, and my classmates were always eager to push me in my wheelchair to lunch, the playground, or wherever we were headed. Of course, there were one or two who made fun of me and my disability, but that didn't last long. Either the teacher stepped in, or one of my classmates was ready to defend me.

THE STRUGGLE FOR NORMALCY

Middle school, however, was tough. Those teenage years were rough, and puberty hit me early, leaving me confused about a lot of things. For example, when I got my period, I had no idea what was happening. Mother didn't talk to us about it, so I was grateful to have older sisters who taught me how to wear a pad—because the first time, I had it sticky side up! That was also the time when all my friends started having boyfriends, and I didn't. I began to notice how different I really was. No boy wanted to be in a relationship with me, and it hurt. I started feeling like I wasn't good enough.

The sadness got to me so much that one day, I took a piece of broken glass from a clock my parents had given me for my birthday and tried to slit my wrist. Thankfully, I didn't cut deep enough. To this day, I can't recall how I got past that dark time. I don't remember anyone talking to me or helping me change my mindset.

THE POWER OF INDEPENDENCE

Towards the end of middle school, I got my first power wheelchair—it was red and black, and I was thrilled to have the independence to get around school and the house on my own. By the time I reached high school, I was an expert driver. Lol. The high school was huge, with hills I loved driving up and down. Just like in earlier years, I had plenty of friends and was well-known. Most people treated me like I was just like them.

Out of all my friends, there were two that I really clung to—they were genuine. I remember one day when my power wheelchair broke down, and my parents had to load me into the car to get me to school. Usually, I took the bus, but that day my old wheelchair from elementary school had to be used. It was brown, with the leg rests coming up to my knees. When I arrived in class and made eye contact with my two friends, we burst into laughter. We laughed so hard throughout the entire class, even though Mrs. Rhea, our sweet teacher, told us to settle down several times. I think we ended up getting written up, but it was just a warning—no detention.

I participated in whatever activities I could during high school, including chorus, 4-H Club, and Student Government. But don't let that fool you about my academic performance—I wasn't one of the "smart" siblings. Not because I couldn't be, but because I was too lazy. Toward the end of high school, my grades were so bad that my mom made me a deal: if I got my grades up and graduated on time, she'd get me my class ring. That was a big deal back then, so I got my grades up and graduated on time. Wow, Thea, you were really something back in the day—and that's not a compliment! Lol.

A NEW SENSE OF STRENGTH

Graduation day felt so special. When my name was called, I rolled across the stage, and as I looked out, the entire auditorium was on their feet, clapping and cheering

My elementary school and class photo.

for me. I was filled with so much joy!

Looking back, I realize how much I've grown and how far I've come since that little girl who learned to write her name, scooted around with her sisters, and tried to fit into a world that didn't always make space for her. From overcoming the doubts of others, navigating through school, and even battling my own insecurities, I've learned that my strength doesn't come from how fast I can move or what I can do on my own —it comes from the love and resilience that was built into me from the very beginning.

It's funny to think how many things I questioned about myself, especially during those tough middle school years. The girl who didn't think she was good enough, who didn't have a boyfriend, who struggled to find her place—she grew into a woman who understands that her value isn't tied to any of those things. Graduation was a special day for me, but in a way, every day after has been a continuation of that celebration. The applause, the support, the love that surrounded me on that stage has stayed with me, pushing me forward, reminding me that I am more than enough. My journey wasn't easy, but it made me who I am today— and for that, I'm incredibly proud.

Chocolate and Peanut Butter Brownies
Kaleshia Holmes

Recipe

Ingredients

4 eggs
2 sticks unsalted butter
1 tsp vanilla flavor
1 cup of all purpose flour
1.5 cups of sugar
8 oz chocolate squares
1/4 cup unsweetened cocoa powder
1/2 tsp salt
1/2 cup creamy peanut butter

Directions

Heat oven to 350

Melt chocolate and butter in a double boiler over medium heat. Stir often and set aside when fully melted and smooth.

In the same bowl stir in the sugar and eggs one at a time

Add vanilla flavor, stir well.

In a separate bowl, mix all-purpose flour, cocoa powder, and salt together.

Add this mixture to the wet ingredient mixture until it is combined.

Pour the batter into a 9x9 greased pan.

Top the batter with spoonfuls of the peanut butter. Take a butter knife and lightly swirl the peanut butter into the batter.

Bake for about 35-40 minutes and let cool before slicing

Jamaican Salt Fish Fritters

Mario Robison

- 1/2 saltfish (cod) hydrated into gallons of water overnight
- 1 1/2 cups of all-purpose flour
- 1/2 teaspoon of baking powder
- 1 small onion finely diced
- Two stocks of green onion chopped
- 1 teaspoon of allspice
- 2 cloves of finely chopped garlic
- 1 tablespoon of Jamaican curry powder
- 1 teaspoon of black pepper
- Pinch of salt to taste
- 1/2 tablespoon of chopped thyme
- 1 cup of water or milk
- Oil for frying (shallow pan)

Chop the fish and mix all ingredients together with the desired thickness of the batter.

Separate and make into patties

Heat oil in the frying pan

Place patties into the pan and fry until golden brown.

PUMPKIN SPICE CUPCAKES

Kayla Brown

Ingredients

1 cup flour
1 teaspoon pumpkin pie spice
1 teaspoon baking powder
1/2 teaspoon baking soda
1/2 teaspoon salt
1/2 teaspoon cinnamon
1 cup pumpkin puree
1/2 cup brown sugar packed
1/2 cup sugar
1/2 cup vegetable oil
2 eggs

Mixing:
1) Prepare cupcake pan with cupcake liners and set aside
2) Set oven to 350 degrees
3) Sift flour, pumpkin pie spice, baking powder, baking soda, and salt together; set aside
4) In a separate mixing bowl, mix oil and sugar
5) Add pumpkin puree
6) Add eggs one at a time
7) Pour in flour mixture; do not over-mix
8) Pour the combined mixture into a cupcake pan and bake for 18-20 minutes

Icing ingredients:
6 tablespoons butter softened
4 ounces of cream cheese softened
2 cups powdered sugar more as needed
1/2 teaspoon vanilla
1 1/2 teaspoons cinnamon (leave off if you want cream cheese frosting only)

Mixing:
1) Cream butter and sugar for approximately 1 minute
2) Add sugar and cinnamon, one cup at a time
3) Add vanilla
4) Mix until smooth

EWKNIKLEE MEE

Dedications

This bio-zine is dedicated to one of the strongest, most determined, and wisest women I have ever known: my mother. She was, and will always remain, unmatched. The person I am today is a direct reflection of her unwavering guidance and tough love. She never allowed me to make excuses for why I couldn't do something, instead challenging me to push beyond my limits. From those long, chastising conversations on the 45-minute drives to Augusta and back, to her firm declaration that if I didn't learn independence, I'd be living with her and Daddy forever, she gave me the motivation I needed to grow.

Her strength was a quiet force—she didn't say much, but her actions spoke volumes. As a mother of nine children, she carried herself with grace, resilience, and an unyielding sense of purpose. She was my biggest supporter in my creative endeavors, always honest and direct. If something wasn't quite right, a simple comment like, "Now, how long did you say this took?" was enough to send me back to the drawing board. :) But when it was good, she'd let me know, not just by telling me, but by proudly sharing my work with her friends, family, and church members. That kind of validation meant everything.

Mother was a true trooper, and her legacy is profound. I pray that I can embody her strength, determination, and love, and become a woman she would be proud of.

Mother, not a day goes by that you don't cross my mind. I carry you with me in a lot that I do. You are truly loved and missed.

This one is for you!

Terrance, you were strong—both mentally and physically—and carried a sense of humor that could brighten any moment. You had a love for RC cars that lit up your face, and a love for me that ran even deeper.

You showed me what it meant to be truly loved outside of my family. Even when you were in the hospital, you worried more about me than yourself, always making sure I was okay. That kind of selflessness is something I'll never forget.

We shared so many fun times, from you pretending to be a preacher just to make me laugh, to you proudly marketing my crafts—even before I knew I had it in me to create anything worth showing off. You believed in me before I believed in myself, and I'll always cherish that.

I thought your new heart would give us so much more time together, and while I wish it had, I know you fought with everything you had. I thank God for every moment we did have and for the lessons you taught me—not only as a person but as a wife.

You loved me to the very end, and I loved you through sickness and health. Your strength, your love, and your belief in me will stay with me forever. 💕

Weapon Formed

SmithBoysRacing
Dedicate Clarence Smith Sr. & Jr.